FRANK

Best wishes
John Chambers

JOHN CHAMBERS

First published in Ireland by
Anchor Productions Limited, Dublin

ISBN: 978-1-910179-54-3

Printed and bound in Ireland
by eprint limited
www.eprint.ie

For my mother

and

In memory of my father

Acknowledgements

To John Killeen whose analysis helped shape this book.

To Joan Lyons for typing the early drafts.

Warm buiochas to Orla Dunne for her support.

To Marguerite Somers, a firm anchor when the going was difficult.

To Anne Chambers for all her advice and encouragement.

Nearest the heart - to Mary, for love expressed in countless ways.

To our daughters, Sarah and Therese.

Foreword

JOHN CHAMBERS has written a fascinating
sequence of sonnets in which ordinary lives achieve
an extraordinary prominence because of the skill
and sheer imaginative tenacity which Chambers
brings to bear on the worlds of Frank, Beth and
others, but especially that of Frank. This is the
contemporary world of "the job", Dublin, home,
family, colleagues, cars, stress, "the hermit
underneath the public skin", golf, death, pubs, sex
and would-be sex. When these sonnets work (and
quite a large number of them work with startling
effectiveness) the reader enters that world evoked
by Chambers with a sensitivity at once both delicate
and tough, compassionate and self-protective. This
is an unusual book, surprising, bleak, perceptive
and memorable; a collection that rewards not just
reading but re-reading.

                                        Brendan Kennelly

Watching Oprah in the dusk, sick at home,
the house around him passive as an ear,
seems under siege. Each hidden creak and groan
is new to him. Perhaps they disappear
when the family pack familiar noise
inside these walls? The programme's on affairs
can they be forgiven and what destroys
a marriage past all possible repairs?
How would Beth react if she dug it out
that he had strayed just recently? The shock
would make her go for blood; there was no doubt
she'd want him gone, proceed to strip him lock
stock and barrel. How people can show their pain
to millions is past him. The gate clicks, she's home again.

Flicking pages of Tony's history book
he makes his way to nineteen forty five.
His birth-date here has stuck him on a hook
to Hiroshima. He became alive
when the A bomb dropped from Enola Gay.
He's linked to doomsday's original sin
to the hour. The text moves on to replay
superpower permafrost and Sputnik's spin
of brief superiority in space,
hope shot down on a Dallas afternoon.
The past's a handicap, a lack of grace
like Armstrong's waddling movement on the moon.
He feels it between the lines, lives each page,
imprisoned by his past, history's cage.

As his drive bullets through the evening sky
down the fairway, he waits for Dominic
to pick his scattered tee. Frank will try
the five on his second shot. Myopic,
it's now another handicap to find
the bloody ball; reliant on his friends.
The worst part of this game is in the mind
with too much time between the strokes. He bends,
eyes the two kidneys of bunker ahead,
sees the perfect shot; knows he is too tight
as he strains for power, his wrist and head
and club are at odds, the ball slices right.
He smiles at Dominic, groans when it finds sand,
seeing perfection once more slip from hand.

In the Longford Arms Hotel, as Frank zipped
up in the Gents, he saw, perfectly clear,
a figure at the hand dryer, and gripped
in a paralysis of shock, not fear,
tried to move, anticipating embrace
of son and long dead father. But his feet
seemed grouted as the tiles below. The face
in profile shifted as if it must meet
his own hungry eyes. Then that full-lipped mouth
parted - preparatory to an advice,
a whispered message or some warning shout?
- closed slowly as the bald head gestured twice
to an unlit Major, then moved from sight.
Left Frank alone, powerless to give light.

A life of heavy food and T.V. lies
in folds about his gut and thighs. He's found
that he's a cheat on diet and exercise
so no longer has a go. But the pound
of nervous heartbeats in the calm of night
contrasts so much with his wife's steady breath.
He gets green headaches from the Apple's light
at work, smells his own undistinguished death
in streaks of red each time he strains to crap,
hungers for signs of universal rust
to ease his own decay. We all take the rap
bluffing through this conspiracy of dust,
knowing nothing lasts, even brilliant sex
for the average man, culminates in secs.

Maeve's voice is steady on the phone, no trace
of pain escapes down this blind instrument.
Although at first Frank's relieved that her face
is out of sight, knowing her temperament
since they were kids, when she could never hide
herself from scrutiny, he feels let down
that his favourite sister won't confide
her feelings as she used to do. They've grown
apart through suffering - there's a silence
between his wholeness and her butchered breast
that can't be crossed by sympathy or sense.
Handicapped by health, he has failed a test
in their relationship. Her calm words show
a fluency, a language he doesn't know.

They wait for him to finish his coffee,
these days it seems he's always catching up.
He feels it with the kids especially,
this lack of pace. He slowly drains his cup
as they share college talk. They'd get along
without this shambling bitter bag of flesh.
For years they were dependent on their strong
dad, a safety net. Now trapped in a mesh
Frank feels passive, uncertain on his feet.
Their world's manic to him, his one defence
is condemnation. They're tuned to the street
treating his stale views with indifference.
"You raise them just to ditch you", he tells Beth.
His gripe sounds like a sour escape of breath.

Now on the Late, Late Show, stripped to the waist,
a long haired Spanish dancer struts his stuff.
Supposed to be a heartthrob – women's taste
is bloody weird. Knowing Beth well enough
he'd bet she'd run miles from this sweaty stud.
He's slower too by far, than Riverdance.
That guy, what was his name, was really good.
Frank stretches his legs, hasn't had a chance
to exercise for weeks, not one full round
since Autumn last. He's on the chubby side,
not that it really matters. He has found
it makes feck all difference. Back inside
the door, Beth watches the foot-tapping punk,
"Oh God" she says, "who is that gorgeous hunk?".

"The greatest human love cannot compare"
said Father Lyons, his sermon done at last,
"with that of God for us". A lifeless stare
is all that Frank gets from his wife. Well past
a week now since she's talked to him at all.
Torn between amusement at this charade
and anger (he's tried his best but can't recall
what set this off, how long it's to be played).
Could be this thing they go through at this age-
she always said she'd love another child?
At other times he feels in her a rage
at their life. He senses her hopes defiled
striking him like a slap across the cheek.
He turns in peace, her handshake's cool and weak.

Sitting across from her, their eyes have met
briefly at certain times, throughout the meal.
When Beth announced she'd asked them, icy sweat
had paralysed his mind. How would he deal
with it before her husband and his wife?
So far he feels it's going well, no slips
in conversation, but he's gripped his knife
so hard his hand is sore, he feels his lips
potential traitors; vows to avoid wine
but finds he drains each glassful in a rush.
His recent lover sitting down to dine
in his home make him want to jump, to crush
the napkin in his fist. He's forced to flee
the scene into the kitchen to make tea.

"I thought that passed off very well", he said
watching greasy water suck down the sink.
Her silence hung between them. Filled with dread
he walked to where she sat "What did you think,
you seemed to enjoy yourself anyway".
He scanned her face, desperate to find clues
behind the even tone and looked away
when her eyes raised upwards. They watched the news
in silence, his mind reeling back the night.
Had he or Anne said something by mistake-
some look? He thought he played it watertight
unless when Anne went in to help Beth make
coffee at the end, could it have spilled out
as a kettle boiled? Frank feels rising doubt.

He used to love the thrill, driving at night,
cats' eyes zapping, machine gunned underneath,
tearing through space, every oncoming light
a planet, collision missed by hair's breath,
left in the wake of Starship Enterprise.
Strange new worlds appeared, lit by amber glows
looming incendiary before the eyes
with unearthly flares in fields and hedgerows.
But that crash outside Youghal really kissed
goodbye to night-time confidence, goodbye
to when he drove at speed, completely pissed
like a drunken comet through the dark sky.
Nervous of night, sober, or on the jar
he grounds himself and lets Beth drive the car.

If Tony was on crack or ecstacy
or a dozen other test tube routes to hell
Frank wonders would he know? The lad seems free
of any signs he's read about, doing well
at school, into soccer, golf, basketball.
Regarding girls, Frank senses he's not slow
on that front. At his son's age the dance hall
was a trial by peers where his awkward show
of interest died against the surge and noise.
The boy seems fine, it's wrong to force the pace.
When they last talked man to man, Tony's poise
shocked him. In calm discussion face to face
on drugs and sex he seemed to know the score,
left Frank mourning innocence's closing door.

Before he reached the mark of fifty years
he'd a check up. "A little overweight"
O'Neill said "but no cause for major fears
as overall the system's in good state.
Heart and blood pressure fine." Could he be wrong?
Frank wondered afterwards but kept it quiet
having heard the expert say he was strong
as a horse. That nightly spurting of bright
red blood in the toilet he decided
not to mention at all. He'd just be moved
for tests, hospitals should be avoided
at all costs; he'd just get tissue removed,
sterile gloves rooting, a pain in the ass;
all for something that will probably pass.

Watching seaspray erupt upon the track
Frank nods and mutters "Yes". It's all Burke needs
to start right off again, no turning back
this deluge of dull detail. The Dart speeds
towards town as Frank contemplates being curt
damming the flood of anecdote and chat
to declare disinterest. The truth would hurt
but he'd have peace commuting after that.
Truth is, it's he himself, not Burke, to blame.
"You're a cold fish, boy" his father once said.
This lack of curiosity is a name
for selfishness, could be he has no head
to absorb other's lives, might be a form
of self-defence. Frank looks out at the storm.

Seeing Anne in the flesh as she stands there
among the mourners at Joe Stafford's grave
unbalances him. Frank feels the shock waves blare
across this discreet place, a tidal wave
in the blood. It seems that Elizabeth
must hear his heartbeats, every single sound
is magnified. At this threshold of death
Anne has paused, standing on the gravelled ground.
Until now, all had been dead and buried,
their mutual mistake; he'd kissed her hair
when they'd laid it all to rest. Now hurried
passion returns to haunt the steady air.
As he stumbles on the straight and narrow
path, his wife turns round, he moves to follow.

"You lack ambition" Beth said yesterday.
Now as he shaves, he's suddenly a boy
again, his future's just the stuff of play
in his own hands, to build or to destroy.
No damage done in this alternate world
he used to think, in cartoon sanctuary
he'd rise above the nonstop setbacks hurled
against him. But nowadays he can see
the weathering of hope across his face,
leaving him no less passive than that glass.
He looks to routine now to set the pace
of his imaginings; to let life pass
seems the proper course, kinder on the brain.
Resigned he smiles into the mirror's pane.

Two fresh school kids on work experience
and he's been picked to steer them round the place.
The girl seems bright but shy, the lad is tense
and Frank, watching them, sees a certain grace,
brittle and fine. Will they be damaged here?
He'd love to shield them against this rough crowd,
the bitter grudging crap which sours the ear
from every desk, repetitious and loud.
Showing them the ropes is the easy part
he realises, they're so keen to learn.
It's the gradual erosions of the heart
he'd love to place before them, and to turn
spotlights on his own decay. No going back.
He just sits tight, rejoins the office crack.

He takes the zap now Beth is on the phone,
presses number three for Match of the Day
and stretches back with a comfortable groan
to hear the three lads dissect tonight's play,
this snug routine every Saturday night.
The second featured match is halfway through
when his wife reappears and seeing him tight
with focus, will not, he knows, ask to view
the film she was watching. And so he hands
the remote over, make the gesture real.
Beth smiles and shakes her head, she understands
the code. This victory always makes him feel
some guilt until his mind moves to the game.
All said and done, for years it's been the same.

How'd they manage if he was on the dole?
The way it's been at work he knows it's not
impossible; life's been on a great roll
for a time now, but it could change. He's got
complacent in the job, works at half speed.
The sale completed doesn't have the thrill
it used to. Time to let the newer breed
all smile and push, and hungry for the kill
take over now? But what's to tempt him out?
His skills, such as they are, too specialised
to survive a transplant. Carrying doubt
with him in the bones, most times it's disguised
except for days like this one, when it grows
like cancer on each thought, and surely shows.

Pausing in the gentle heat this Easter Day
he feeds the Aga; Beth's upstairs in bed.
The anthracite rattles, how can one weigh
the cost of telling her against the dread
of someone adding to the fire he's set?
But either way, no matter how it breaks
she'll have the moral ground, she'll make him sweat.
She'll never understand his hot mistakes.
Better to hide all tracks, the evidence,
in written form at least, is slim. He throws
Anne's two letters, sniffing her faint fragrance
one final time before the Aga claws
in those few lines of infidelity.
Passion burnt down, he's left with memory.

This year they'll travel by themselves to France.
Tony agreed to come reluctantly
last time and Frank can't blame him for his stance
he just needs time to himself. Beth can see
only rejection, the family split
apart, first time since nineteen seventy four.
Women feel that the pieces have to fit
long past the point of no return. At core
Frank does feel tiny stirrings of unease,
both chickens flown the coop. Left on their own,
what have they now to go on with but tease
old worries, pick at problems, gnaw the bone
of quarrels for the sake of it? They're freed
to probe their marriage, let each other bleed.

He could be a rapist, she's not to know
what makes this strange anonymous male tick.
The girl sits in beside him, thighs on show
'till she re-arranges dress. His eyes flick
on her cleavage as he pretends to check
in the rear mirror's impure glass. He feels
like a teenager, not giving a feck
a woman by his side, a set of wheels.
Newman, Dean or Brando, he slowly drives
through this familiar town. Spotted at lights
by Ed and Jarlath waiting for their wives
to quit the gab, he mimes carnal delights.
She's young, bored and dumb. His fantasies fall.
She never thanks him for the lift at all.

"Although it's been six weeks since Stephen died
there are nights, especially nights, I feel he's here
beside me. Can you understand"? Frank lied
nodding affirmation, desperate to steer
their talk to safer ground, feels his replies
are weak and clumsy. "Sure it's for the best".
A flash of anger in her widowed eyes
masked by a smile. All he can do is jest
and sell. He drains his glass, the welcome burn
of whiskey, for a minute, stuns the doubt.
Useless at comforting, not one to turn
to in crisis time. But on his way out
he is astonished when he hears her say
"You're great Frank, you have really changed my day."

A new habit, lunching alone these days
away from Casey's endless moans and sneers,
or Donovan's backhanded spurts of praise
at Frank's record over seventeen years.
Frank likes the sense of independent quiet
sitting in city centre pubs, with time
to vegetate on a microwaved diet.
Solitude for an hour is sublime.
He begrudges returning here at two
as if from holidays. Begins to feel
the same on the domestic front, too few
minutes to himself; feels he has to peel
off all contact, to find himself again,
this hermit underneath the public skin.

That's the third night running that Beth has called
the same name in her sleep. Frank knows no Joe
except for Joe Dineen, grumpy and bald
and six feet under now, that Beth might know.
Tonight again, she calls the name, then cries
while Frank, feeling her sobbing at his back,
(they've always slept as spoons) wonders what lies
in her dream world. He feels a sudden lack
gnaw at his rest, there is this secret place
he is excluded from. He'd love to shake
her from her furtive sleep, get her to face
the knowledge that he knows. He stays awake
a lifetime as she sinks to silent sleep
out of his reach, her secret buried deep.

And all because the lady loves Milk Tray.
Watching the guy delivering chocolates
Frank suddenly remembers yesterday
was his sister's birthday. Now he's too late
to even send a card. How did he forget
this year of all, her with breast surgery
just a month ago? She'll be quite upset
if he knows Maeve. He might call out to see
her tomorrow afternoon, they could lunch
together in the Gallery, like old days.
He'll lay it on to make it up, a bunch
of roses might just do the trick. It pays
to go the extra bit when you're behind.
He nods, this plan of action soothes his mind.

"Location is where it's at" he declares.
The girl looks blank, but he gets down payment
of a smile from her husband. Going upstairs
her legs are drop dead beauts, without a doubt
the highlight of this lousy day so far.
Two sales collapsed, his game of golf postponed,
then to cap it, a ticket on the car
right outside the office too; Dempsey stoned
again - his number must be up. He'd love
to tell this young lad to take this flat
off his hands, clear his desk, a career move
straight to the dole. Walk off a lifetime's fat.
Right now he'd swap anything just to be
between these thighs. Location is the key.

"God, that was some case, Frank, that priest last week",
Jordan said "dying in that gay sex place.
The more you think of it, if flesh is weak
enough the best will fall. How did he face
his congregation over all those years
especially at Confessions. , there's the bit
I can't follow?" Frank hesitates and steers
the talk to safer ground, knowing he could fit
the questions neatly into his own life.
So much deceit to trip him up, it seems
at times amazing that he's kept his wife
and kids at all. His sins are like bad dreams
that come back at times, though he sleeps secure
most nights. Keeping things in place is the cure.

Standing alone he pours another glass
of gin. Hard to believe. He cannot think
of George being dead. Traffic lights after Mass,
massive heart attack on green. In a blink
a life is gone, yet Frank just feels remote.
A mirror above the fire shows his eyes
unemotional and set. He clears his throat,
glass in his hand, then shakes his head and sighs
and gulps his third. Might as well get tight
with nothing left to do, the mourners gone.
Beth's upstairs with Pauline, she'll stay the night
with them, she couldn't think of being alone
without George, his unidentical twin.
He pours, seeking the sour release of gin.

They walk apart on this familiar strand
remembering a summer, their first time there.
He'd shown her Ireland's Eye and with his hand
pointing due north told her that on a clear
day the Mountains of Mourne could just be seen,
and showed her where to look. He loved being guide,
this form of leading at a dance, the sheen
of pleasure in her eye she couldn't hide.
Now a low cloud bank rolls in from Lambay
obscuring everything. He cannot see
a way of telling her the truth, no way
would she forgive, best course is secrecy.
He's relieved, visibility's improved.
The option taken is right, clouds have moved.

Her birthday and Beth wanted to stay in.
Now Frank sits breathing in the Giorgio
a present from their son. She leaves her gin
untouched, looking as if she'd love to go
home now. She turns away, again the whiff
of perfume as she moves. Can women smell
betrayal? Their talk is awkwardly stiff
the meal upstairs hangs like a prison spell.
He feels appetite shrivel as they dine
predicting their night ahead; dull remarks
on other diners, service, food or wine.
She'll hit the ladies at least twice, forced sparks
of gaiety if they happen to meet friends.
Thrown back on each other, excitement ends.

Advised to walk, he's found new routes at lunch
and resting with a Yorkie yesterday
past Leeson Street Bridge on a canal bench
he sees them in the grass, a slow foreplay
of twisting jeans, her hand inside his fly.
In urban day, oblivious they move
as languid as the water lazing by
and watching from the other bank young love
he feels a bile of lust and envy surge
into his mind, remembering as a teen
a few rare chances, when despite the urge
he couldn't contemplate at all being seen.
He moves away, depressed by sense of waste,
leaving the bar behind him, he's lost taste.

Feeling an urge for weeks to clear the slate
he crosses the city to Clarendon Street.
It's years since the last time, unhealthy weight
presses on his brain - considers retreat
right up to the moment he joins the queue.
Remembering the drill he kneels and tries
to rehearse a list, slides along the pew
as the door clicks open, so many lies
the affair with Anne, drunken arguments.
It's chair to chair, no covering darkness here.
The young priest nods, Frank feels his memory tense
and knows that he must leave, he cannot share
his private brutal world with this fresh face.
He turns abruptly, shuts the door on grace

Twenty years to this day, the old man died.
Frank had done an interview, meant to call
into the ward, but got snared, then blindeyed
drunk with John Muldoon, a six hour pub crawl.
Beth broke the news on his scattered head
brimming with beer and gin. She took the wheel,
giving out as they broke lights. He was dead
five minutes when they arrived, Frank could feel
their disapproval. His indulgence stank
the room. George was there with Maeve and Margaret.
Touching his stiffening face he felt his rank
as number one fall back. Yet he'd have bet
Dad would've smiled, he loved his jar each night
'till cancer's hunger killed all appetite.

The camera pans across these starving hordes
a wide angle shot, taken from above
Goma's refugee camp. Frank leans towards
the set in despair. When push comes to shove
how could one God manage to take this in,
with individual love there for all?
Not for the first time Frank feels his faith spin
round to an instinct that we too will fall,
as billions who have sunken into clay
before us fell, to stern mortality.
All those horrors, impossible to say
that He could stand aside and leave us free
to wage atrocities, and in His name:
infinitely blind, letting man take blame.

Right down the shoulders, back and upper thigh
it happened at the long fifteenth, on tee.
Straining for distance he'd really let fly
sacrificing direction, totally
off course in rough. With contact came a spear
of agony which lasted for a week,
seven long days dominated by the fear
of what he'd done, when bending for a leak
was a test of nerves. The future will hold
so many other dangers. If the strain
is showing now, what happens when he's old,
handicapped by infirmity and pain?
Years stretch ahead, he hopes to play the pole
get good position for that final hole.

Beth is out at her prayer group tonight.
She's just joined. This week's theme, the notice said,
was marriage. Good material there all right
if she talks from experience. No bed
of roses for them both; she suffered most
hours of lonely housework, minding the kids
while he binged, blazed away at golf, the cost
building up, their relationship on skids,
empty as a husk. She tried, he was tired
of endless new beginnings, each replay
of renewed peace then arguments inspired
only boredom. His fling with Anne a stray
and minor ingredient in the pot,
blending with years' accumulated rot.

Buttoning up later, if Frank had a wish
it would be to rewind the last half hour,
erase every bit from start to finish,
from where she opened the apartment door.
All wiped from sight, the condom's swollen purse,
his climax, abrupt and numb, her massage
on the leather couch, the panting black nurse
on video, the money paid. A rage
burns his head as he considers again
for this he's risked his marriage, maybe life,
Aids, the law, loss of job, all just to gain
a spasm of release! What of his wife,
if she guessed? For this is not the first time,
add his affair to boot, he's only slime.

Just how his fragile wife has learned to cope
he cannot understand : her mother cold
and remote, asking Beth her name, no hope
of recovery once it's taken hold.
For five years now he's marvelled at her nerve
facing this detached mind that sense has fled.
The occasional memories just serve
to show how much is lost. The doctors said
she could last for years, nobody can tell.
Beth spends hours at a time with her. A long
ten minutes stretched like a malignant spell
tonight leaves Frank feeling he doesn't belong.
He cuts his visit short, inventing chores
to her heedless ears, breathes outside the door.

Image after image breaks ceaselessly
and Frank, channel surfing just to unwind,
begins to half appreciate the free
uncluttered security of the blind.
If there's a God with unrestricted view
what does he make of it all through this pane,
this window on the world, a daily spew
of flotsam? Must be times He'd like to drain
the clogged up sink, undo the nightly trap
assert control, clear this polluted screen?
A single press of a heavenly zap
would do the job and leave creation clean.
Still for free will's sake, He won't interfere
tonight, Frank hopes, with kick off time so near?

At times he feels he's never learned the code
of real communication. Take today's
discussion with Tony on school which flowed
sluggishly for ten minutes. The lad stays
with Beth another hour. Frank feels to blame,
hearing the murmur upstairs as he sits
watching the News. With Karen it's the same
their talk just trails away in awkward fits.
It's Beth who starts and fleshes out the chats
they have. He's lost except for arguments
on sport or politics with friends, and that's
distant from what he feels, just stuff he rents
from other people's views, papers, T.V.
Regurgitating rubbish endlessly.

Six years married before Karen was born
they'd been on the verge of adopting one.
It was as if sex needed a return
on their invested effort. When he'd come
the thoughts would surge up; was this just a blank
again, who was at fault, was his seed spilled
on barren soil? George, who told him to thank
his lucky stars, had five kids. Sex was killed
for Eoin and Ruth, she couldn't use the Pill.
Now out of the production trap with two,
it seems perverse that neither has the will
to move except on rarest nights, this new
abstinence seems to suit them both; a show
of real content, or old age down below?

"Everyone past the thirty five year mark
needs them", Tom Belton said, as the lens slid
through the empty test frame. Magically stark
letters were revealed that before now hid
beyond his clench of squinting sight, yet he
knows this new look will soon necessitate
a badge, a mark of ageing plain to see.
"Spectacles are high fashion, you'll look great"
Beth reassured him when they met outside.
"You'll be distinguished, glasses and grey hair".
But Frank feels sealed from youth. Now he can't hide
from view this see through sign of wear and tear.
Unless he bluffs his way and tries to lie;
a myopic world, less than meets the eye.

Twenty eight years married today (Frank's the one
who remembers their anniversaries)
and even though straight from the starter's gun
they'd felt the going tough, a certain ease
developed, smoothing out sharp novelty
- less jockeying for place. He'd kept tight rein
on lust, confined, in case of number three
to rare safe nights. Times, justified by strain
he'd paid for sex in town, then that weekend
with Anne at the Blue Haven in Kinsale.
Otherwise no secrets, save what he'd spend
on those well fancied favourites, bred to fail.
Marriage needs these gambles, adds spice to life,
bound to be flutters between man and wife.

"Observe, Remember, Learn". Thought for the day
on the calendar. Shaving, Frank can see
lines of threatening low lying clouds, some grey
bird lifting slowly off the neighbour's tree.
Patting his chin, it hits him suddenly
that he seldom examines things, at best
he's blurred on detail, lacks the energy
or will to store up facts. He's flunked each test
of remembering names, faces that he's met
before, a sign he doesn't give a damn
for other peoples' lives, a pattern set
from a self-absorbed youth? "It's bad to cram
fine brains with junk," he jokes, "it's self abuse".
Beth smiles, he knows she sees through his excuse.

Coming back from Bernies, he takes the wheel.
He's had a fair few vodkas and white wine
and that pissy apple punch, but the meal
has soaked it up. They had a lovely time.
Beth is on a high, her evening's been made
by the bracelet he bought her Tuesday last.
Admired all night. If she knew guilt had paid
the deposit there. That's all in the past.
In neutral, waiting at a long red light
he leans across, and kisses her cool cheek.
Later she moves above him clawing tight
across his chest. Her passion leaves him weak
so that he comes, long afterwards, feels sure
punishment's just deferred for the impure.

48

He's learned to cope, can do some basic things
on the Mackintosh, click up properties
that they have on their books, the market swings,
an in-house list of customers, the fees
unpaid. But beyond these functions he stands
on unsurveyed ground. He's no hunger now,
nor ever will, to go beyond demands
of work. There's no machine can tell you how
to nudge a sale without being seen to push.
He watches the younger ones idly play,
producing graphs and print outs in a gush
of colour; natural with it in a way
he'll never be. An innocent at sea
among slick surfers of technology.

Frank loves browsing in the video store,
the smell of warm plastic, the films empty
on shelves, the sense of there being much more
than meets the eye, this stripped down secrecy
is exciting. He knows it's wrong to judge
by cover, yet he gets a thrill to stall
holding a skin flick, yet not cross the ledge
and take it out at the desk. Overall
on taste, he and Beth don't see eye to eye.
She could keep going on a steady flow
of big star hits, courtroom trials and old spy
movies with romance thrown in, while he'd go
for laughs, or occasionally rent a few
to watch (if Beth was out) completely blue.

The more he thinks about it looking back
the more he sees how risky it became,
as it progressed, the less they covered track.
It was as if a tiredness with the game
set in, no buzz in perfect secrecy.
They began to take risks, he'd wait until
Beth neared the phone before he'd say goodbye.
Other times they'd rendezvous for the thrill
outside the house. However, day by day,
the lure of staying just one step ahead
began to fade. The price they had to pay
cancelled out the sporadic joy in bed.
So they agreed, to mutual relief,
to finish the affair, no blame, no grief.

Frank's driving because of Beth's fractured wrist.
He made a sacrifice - two before lunch
scarcely touched the wine. Last year he was pissed
before they reached the dessert stage, that punch
was pure volcanic stuff. He still feels tense
as he slugs on through the lane-hopping fight
for open road. These days it's an offence
to sniff the bloody stuff, the roads at night
with three weeks to Christmas have been alive
with guards. He's been breathalized twice, in luck
on both counts. It can kill - to drink and drive
a billboard blares. He knows by Beth's grim look
that he has failed to keep this morning's pledge.
Another break in trust, another wedge.

That week-end break at Halloween was great
just what they needed - his suggestion too.
It's like they're in the way back there of late
just an open house with friends of their two
nonstop socialites who must entertain
at home every second night. At their age
- no he's promised Beth he'll drop that refrain
in the cause of peace and turn a new page.
Accept them as they are, so civilised.
But what about our need for privacy
he grumbled, half asleep and satisfied
after love, (their last time was February).
Ready to promise anything he knows
morning softens out the strongest vows.

Why exactly he keeps the faith he can't
explain clearly to O'Shea. Even though
at times he's felt out of tune with the cant
and intrigue of the Church, he can't let go.
For years giving example to the kids
was a prop he leaned on, a shored up stance
which came in useful with the many skids
of bad luck in his life. He learned to dance
cautiously, conscious of the rules on floor
and glad of the limits, like a safe waltz
an insurance scheme to be kept in store
for wet eternity, allowing faults.
An all-forgiving God was just the pill
to stanche doubt's haemorrhage each day might spill.

After years of selling its poor goodbye,
passionless tributes, set of clubs and clock;
removed from view, a condemned property.
Frank sees his own forced exit, taking stock
after Paddy Maguire's retirement do.
Now he trawls the square, indicator light
kerbing for a lark, desire pushing through
below as she bends, top and mini tight
to the car in front. Frank knows that same heat
burning ahead. Tonight he'd love to dip
in anonymous relief but he'll meet
the lads in Toners, knows the night will slip
to soft office yarns, when the tiny print
is the cruise for loveless sell, hard as flint.

The black couple are so suave, awkwardly
Frank forces himself to effusive chat.
He's relieved when they move upstairs to see
the bedrooms in this luxury city flat.
He feels uptight; could be those Loyalists
he heard, while driving, on the radio
beneath their bland talk their primitive fists.
Now these two, mustn't let his dislike show.
Absently he turns towards a calendar,
where slant-eyed nudes straddle a beam of wood.
He wills himself to rise into a spar
- a month of fun, until a sudden thud
in the hall, brings him back to gracious state,
smiling broadly, smooth salesman of estate.

This evening, on Verbena Avenue
Frank sees, out of the corner of his eye,
(made more intimate through uncurtained view)
an indoor scene that stops him driving by.
He pulls up alongside a lawn to stare
through bay windows where at a Christmas tree
stand man and boy, the adult on a chair.
A string of bulbs between them brilliantly
connects their figures in a chain of light,
illuminating one uplifted face
radiant in openmouthed delight.
Haunted by memory, Frank leaves the place
with a sense of loss. Driving off again
he sees himself and Tony through that pane.

Marooned here in this hot department store,
he hears her "Hi Dad" on the moving stairs
as she glides to view from the second floor
to where he waits, conscious between the pairs
of marbled garden nudes. In that instant
of her breathless kiss, fragrant on his face
he is catapulted back - a distant
memory unwinds. In this very place
sixteen years ago, he'd brought her to see
Switzer's window for the first time, then here
to pick up gloves for Beth, then suddenly
realised she'd left his side. Ten minutes fear
before they'd found her at a jewellery stand.
Now he resists the urge to hold her hand.

The priest advised that he should make amends
repair the fractured trust, avoid the sin,
ignore 'this woman', or meet just as friends
in company, and that he should begin
a new beginning with his wife, a love
without condition, ask nothing in advance.
He'd done his best, since he'd confessed, to move
his own desires back, but Beth's cold stance
makes him think again. A casual fling,
not worth the guilt that's had him by the balls.
He's been supportive since he wore the ring.
Perfect men are saints, so perhaps he falls
the odd time on the way, but to his mind
agreements built on total trust are blind.

The rumour is that Billy's for the chop.
His sales have fallen three years in a row
and yet Frank knows, the man was going non stop
up to lately. Frank reckons he must know
the score, all he can feel is sympathy
for this tight figure, clenched as a fist.
The job has him drained of laughs, he's empty
of all enjoyment. Seeing him dully pissed
at the Christmas 'do, wife as hard as brass
bitching about their life to embarrassed ears,
Frank remembers a carefree lad in class
and views the weathering of forty years
stress and strain. He finds Billy hard to face,
knowing he too could face a fall from grace.

He's made a promise to himself he'll try
to make her rest, relax on Christmas Day.
She's been exhausted recently, with high
blood pressure to boot, yet again the day
begins with him outsleeping her in bed.
He wakes to breakfast tray, fires set downstairs
at least Karen is on hand slicing bread
and salmon. Tony takes him unawares,
arranging crystal glasses and the drink
and dips. He's beaten to the door as well
- it's the Traceys. Before he's time to think
a vodka's in his hands and turkey smell
wafts around him. He pours another one.
Now all's in order, everything is done.

Visiting his father's grave on Christmas Day
Frank notices the weeds that have emerged
between the marble chip stones; Nature's way,
refusing to be smoothed or submerged.
Like the old man himself, to stay in place
had been a challenge to his restless style.
How did he stick the stagnant daily pace
of small town marriage, peacetime like a file
on his brittle energy? In the dead
of night Frank had so often heard his screams.
"Your father fought the Tans", his mother said
when he'd ask. He'd nod, imagining dreams
of bloody ambushes crack through the nights.
He bends to tug the grasses out of sight.

On this very date, a St. Stephen's night
party at Jack McGrath's they had first met.
A dance or two, they chatted, in those slight
exchanges he knew something strong was set.
He'd dropped her at her house, then driving back
with Mickser in the rear, the wipers stuck
and grating on the iced-up glass, a track
of car tyres in the snow, he'd chanced to look
and saw behind a silhouetted hill
a star, like a spurting match, blaze earthward.
It seemed a portent then, he watched until
it disappeared. Tonight there's not one word
between them on that same road. He keeps his eye
on potholes, under a nondescript sky.

Now since it's finished, he's become aware
in a way that's never entered his mind
before he set his sights on this affair,
of what he's almost lost. His lust was blind
but now, like when his mother's cataracts
came out, she'd seen such detail in her room,
so Frank now knows how near the edge his acts
have brought the family. A sense of doom
averted, has focused him to repay
the damage he hopes Beth will never know
he's caused. If non stop care's the price to pay
then he'll pay that price, make the marriage grow
despite his past. He's sure it can be built
to strength, through the corrective lens of guilt.

Each New Years Eve, in optimistic youth
he'd made out lists, determined to improve
his mind or build up muscle, keep the truth
firm in his sights, set targets so he'd prove
that progress was being made. Now as he stands
at fifty, pale and plump before the glass
made blind by steam except where with his hands
he's rubbed a clearing, he sees how he has
let go, those shortcomings he'd tried to kill
repeat like daily stubble on his face.
This has it's own reward, he knows, the thrill
of stupid ambitions life puts in place.
He knows himself well, at this old year's end;
clears a glassy grin, reveals an old friend.